the little book of e

by e. ethelbert miller

with hebrew translations by rafi ellenson

City Point Press

Paperback ISBN: 978-1-947951-72-3
eBook ISBN: 978-1-947951-73-0

First edition

Published by City Point Press
www.citypointpress.com
Distributed by Simon and Schuster
For sales inquiries, contact Simon & Schuster (866) 506-1949
For rights inquiries, contact City Point Press (203) 349-8413

Cover and book design by Barbara Aronica
Manufactured in the United States of America

The author wishes to thank the D.C. Commission on the Arts and Humanities for helping him find the time to write this book.

For David Ellenson

My heart stirs with pretty words

I speak my poem to a king

My language is the pen of a skilled scribe

רָחַשׁ לִבִּי דָּבָר טוֹב
אֹמֵר אָנִי מַעֲשַׂי לְמֶלֶךְ
לְשׁוֹנִי עֵט סוֹפֵר מָהִיר:

Psalms 45:2

תְּהִלִּים מה:ב

introduction

Ethelbert gifted me his words and trusted me to turn them into Hebrew. I riffed on them—as translation is another form of jazz and adopts the same language of theme and variation. It occupies the same space as John Coltrane taking the theatrical beauty of "My Favorite Things" and turning it into a "whirling dervish." My work on these poems started as an exercise that my poetry teacher—the wonderful Joanna Chen—offered me on a March day over a spinach bourekas and iced coffee. "See what you can do with this," she said. I dove into Ethelbert's poetry. I devoured his biography. His beginnings in the Bronx, his career that straddled the line of academic and author, his connection to many major writers of the 20th century, his vocation as a literary activist, and his dedication to bridging divides through literature. I found it—and continue to find it—a privilege to translate his words into Hebrew. As a white Jew, on a more personal note, I am moved by Ethelbert's consistent dedication to dialogue between and within Black and Jewish communities throughout his career.

Translating Ethelbert's poetry from English to Hebrew was an immense and rewarding challenge that I will not soon forget. Not least among the challenges was that

Hebrew is not my native language. Following the structured but generative format of haiku provided another set of obstacles that I was eager to learn how to manage with delicacy and grace. In both of these charges, questions of authenticity and authorial intent abounded. To whom was I being most faithful to in any given moment—Ethelbert, the Hebrew poem, or the Modern Hebrew language? The task became clear. In every moment I had to be true to all of these different voices, while also creating a cohesive aesthetic sense throughout the collection. Learning to do this was a practice as serious as a jazz musician practicing their scales, a poet reading up on the canon, and myself learning as much as I could about Ethelbert, the art of haiku, and Modern Hebrew so as to be a proper translator sensitive to these three components. Consider this haiku:

88
where is my jazz hat
the one that monk used to wear
oh ruby my dear

כּוֹבַע גֵ׳ז שֶׁלִּי
זֶה שֶׁמּוֹנְק הָיָה חוֹבֵשׁ
רוּבִּי יְקָרָה

On first read, this poem appears to be a tribute to the great jazz pianist Thelonious Monk. Known for wearing many radical examples of headgear including colorful skullcaps, trillbies, berets, and more, it is indeed a fair question to ask where have all of Monk's hats gone? Then, Ethelbert leaves no doubt as to who he might be describing when he alludes to the Monk tune, "Ruby, My Dear" in the last line (in fact, it would be a worthy project to create a compilation mix of all the wonderful songs Ethelbert makes reference to throughout this collection). However, knowing Ethelbert's biography pays off here as the double meaning of the second line creates another sense of the line—and the poem—altogether. Ethelbert has written about his late brother Richard who had become a literal monk prior to his premature death. Knowing this adds another layer to the poem. Could this poem be using the language of Monk's music to discuss Ethelbert's longing for his brother? The charge for myself as a translator is how to bring this consonant dissonance—this question— into the Hebrew itself. It seemed inappropriate to translate the word monk into its Hebrew equivalent—נָזִיר, *nazeer*— as it comes with its own associations that Ethelbert surely did not intend in English. Ultimately, I decided to transliterate the word, and the name, Monk into Hebrew—מוֹנְק, *monk*—as I felt it could best encapsulate all the different meanings I understood in the poem, especially after conversation with Ethelbert about the poem.

This fits into a broader conversation about Hebrew aesthetics. To translate this collection appropriately, I had to regularly ask whether the artistic sense of the Hebrew matched that of the English in tone, quality, and beauty. Part of my job as a translator is to choose one specific word, out of many options, to gift to you, the reader, while the other choices languish in my notebook and in computer files of rough drafts. And, in turn, you may why I chose a certain word over another. All of these choices must rely on a dedication and fidelity to an artistic vision established by the source language, English, that will be executed in the target language, Hebrew. As such, even the nature of this project fit into the form of jazz haiku that Ethelbert sought to capture in this collection's poetry. For example:

13
so dizzy the world
climate change sparks new jazz
can you dance to it

דִּיזִי הָעוֹלָם
שִׁנּוּי אַקְלִים מַצִּית
גֵ'ז - לֵךְ תִּרְקְדוּ

This poem proved especially challenging, not for its syllables, but because there were so many options that seemed fitting, especially considering the source poem's wordplay. Similar to the Monk poem above, I had to contend with multiple layers in the English that were inherent to the specific word choice. In this case, the wordplay would be more obvious to a casual reader, so it demanded a different type of focus and care—not more or less, simply another type of surgeon's scalpel. Here Dizzy is trumpeter Dizzy Gillespie as well as the state of the world amidst the pains of climate change. Jazz Haiku is typified by describing the state of the modern world and particularly the lens of Black experience through the poetic means of haiku. This poem asks what it might mean to look at the world through the work of a bandleader who was a virtuoso and self-taught musician with large, puffy cheeks. The perfect imperfection of his jazz. Can we dance to it? Capturing these nuances demanded the question, do I include the Hebrew word for dizzy in this poem— מְסַחְרֵר , *misachr er*—but ultimately I did not because I determined the name, identifying with the character of Gillespie, was of more importance. The semantic meaning of the word— דִיזִי , dizzy—would shine through in Hebrew as well and be truer to the wordplay that Ethelbert sought out to make.

When I began this project, I had a particular conception of the role Hebrew would play. I situated this project in the grand history of American Hebraist literature of the first half of the 20th Century or, rather, as part of the revival of such. In recent years, Yiddish-language literature and artistic expression have experienced a major resurgence in North America and it is my hope that Modern Hebrew can have a similar renewal here. In order for that to be the case, American Modern Hebrew literature must reflect American interests and American questions. Ethelbert's collection, in English, among other themes, reflects uniquely American concerns and Black American concerns at that. It is crucial to understand that this collection emerged amidst the social uprising of 2020 and its follow up protests against white supremacy. Translating these ideas into Hebrew definitionally creates a Hebrew language—an American Hebrew language—for American ideas. The below haiku exemplifies this.

60
early morning walk
it seems the world is still here
black lives still matter

צְעָדַת שַׁחַר
נִדְמֶה הָעוֹלָם עוֹד כָּאן
וּבְלַאק לַייבז מַאטֶר

Thrice in this collection, Ethelbert employs the vital slogan Black Lives Matter. The question of how to translate the phrase into Hebrew is a complicated one, but ultimately lends itself to the ongoing development of an American Hebrew. One option could be to literally translate the term—חַיִּים שְׁחוֹרִים עֲדָיִין נֶחְשָׁבִים, *Black Lives Still Matter*—but this is both clunky and does not fit the syllable requirements!

It's worthwhile to see how similar questions of an American Hebrew play out in a non-transliterated context as well.

4

oh- noise in my yard
robins bluejays and cardinals
the sky has no wings

אוֹשָׁה בֶּחָצֵר
קַרְדִּינָל עוֹרְבָן כָּחֹל
אַךְ בְּלִי כְּנָפַיִם

Not only, as aforementioned, did this book emerge out of the 2020 uprisings, but this book is inseparable from the context of the ongoing COVID-19 pandemic. In fact, this book, the titular little book of e, began as a tiny composition book that Ethelbert started to write in during the early days of the pandemic. This poem relates an experience of being trapped inside and seeing an external, natural world that continues to live on. For the sake of the freeing and limiting syllable count, I was unable to directly translate the third line and so I had to be more interpretive and constructive—with Ethelbert's approval. The third line of this poem in Hebrew translates to "but without wings." In this way, the image of the sky has been lost, but priority has been given to the image of the wings. My decision was inspired by the fact that the emotive sense of the haiku lay within the wings—the idea of flight and of escape.

My hope is that this book, with English and Hebrew side-by-side, can function as a prayerbook of sorts. One that allows for transcending the current problematic state of things, flying past the plague of COVID-19, racism, and anti-semitism. I pray this will be a collection of poetry that will serve not only as an antidote, but a tool and testament to the best of what translation can do—both enhancing the original and acting as stand-alone poems. May this book follow—in Ethelbert's continued tradition of literary activism, the Hebrew language's storied tradition of aesthetics, and the haiku's legacy of brevity.

—Rafi Ellenson

the little book of e

1

oh– water sundays

our spirits need to be washed

let us learn to walk

מֵי יְמֵי רִאשׁוֹן
יֵשׁ לִטְבֹּל נִשְׁמוֹתֵינוּ
לִלְמֹד לָלֶכֶת

2

to wed in summer

everything green is blooming

butterflies take vows

חֲתֻנָּה קֵיצִית
כָּל הַיָּרֹק צוֹמֵחַ
נִדְרֵי פַּרְפָּרִים

3

so dark the new day

a burning sky so tongueless

hush of dead flowers

כֹּה כֵּהֶה הַיּוֹם
שָׁמַיִם לוֹהֲבִים אִלְמִים
לַחַשׁ הַכְּמִישָׁה

4

oh– noise in my yard

robins bluejays and cardinals

the sky has no wings

אוֹשָׁה בַּחֲצַר
קַרְדִּינָל עוֹרְבָן כָּחֹל
אַךְ בְּלִי כְּנָפַיִם

5

bronx housing projects
the birds always flew higher
our dreams with short arms

שְׁכוּנֵי הַבְּרוֹנְקְס
צִפּוֹרִים עָפוּ מַעְלָה
הַחֲלוֹם קְצַר יָד

6

rake broom in the yard
high mounds of leaves around me
sweat– the sound of work

גּוֹרֵף בֶּחָצֵר
תְּלֵי עָלִים מִסָּבִיבִי
זֵעָה - קוֹל עָמָל

7

oh the buddha sits

his hands in a form of prayer

the path is not here

הוֹ בּוּדְהָה יוֹשֵׁב

כַּפָּיו נוֹשֵׂא בִּתְפִלָּה

הַשְּׁבִיל אֵינוֹ כָּאן

8

how lonely my arms

trees walk away from the wind

i now hold nothing

זְרוֹעוֹתַי בּוֹדְדוֹת

עֵצִים בּוֹרְחִים מֵרוּחַ

בְּיָדַי אֵין כְּלוּם

9

moonlight on the floor

the stars are missing tonight

the room is empty

עַל רִצְפָּה סַהַר
הַלַּיְלָה אֵין כּוֹכָבִים
הַחֶדֶר מְרֻקָּן

10

when she falls asleep

all her dreams are shared with me

daybreak is so hard

כְּשֶׁהִיא נִרְדֶּמֶת
חֲלוֹמוֹתֶיהָ אֶצְלִי
אָז שַׁחַר קָשֶׁה

11

the cat wags its tail

rising it moves with such grace

oh, hear the night purr

הֶחָתוּל מְכַשְׁכֵּשׁ

הַזָּנָב נָע בְּחֵן מֻפְלָא

הוֹ! גִּרְגּוּר לֵילִי

12

is it groundhog day

we put on our black cloth masks

hide until we vote

הַכִּבָּר פֶּבְּרוּאָר

שִׂים מַסֵּכֶת בַּד שְׁחוֹרָה

עַד שֶׁנַּצְבִּיעַ

13

so dizzy the world

climate change sparks new jazz

can you dance to it

דִיזִי הָעוֹלָם
שִׁנּוּי אַקְלִים מַצִּית
גֶ׳ז - לֵךְ תִּרְקְדוּ

14

yes a love supreme

Coltrane places horn to lips

beauty out of man

אַהֲבָה עִלִּית
קוֹלְטְרֵיְן, קֶרֶן עַל שְׂפָתוֹ
יוֹפִי בְּצַלְמוֹ

15

lush life disappears
now will you take the a-train
I love you madly

לְלֹא חֶדְוַת חַיִּים
הֲתִקְחִי רַכֶּבֶת a
אוֹהֵב עַד אֵין קֵץ

16

sidewalks wet from rain
clouds no longer wear their shoes
let's jump the puddle

מִדְרָכוֹת גְּשׁוּמוֹת
הָעֲנָנִים הַיְחֵפִים
נְדַלֵּג עַל שְׁלוּלִית

17

squirrels dart about
oak branches sway with laughter
now the week begins

סְנָאִים מִתְרוֹצְצִים
עָנָף אַלּוֹן נָד צוֹחֵק
שָׁבוּעַ מַתְחִיל

18

spring will cry again
sirens outside the window
blues walk in new york

אָבִיב שׁוּב יִבְכֶּה
צְפִירָה מְחוּץ לַחַלּוֹן
הַבְּלוּז בָּנְיוּ יוֹרְק

19

your hair turns silver

the waves cresting at the beach

grains of sand endless

שְׂעָרֵךְ מַכְסִיף
גַּל מִתְנַפֵּץ אֶל הַחוֹף
יָם וָחוֹל לְלֹא סוֹף

20

hug the open sky

flowers bloom when they are loved

see cardinals flying

חַבֵּק רָקִיעַ
לְעֵת הָאַהֲבָה פְּרִיחָה
עָף הַקַּרְדִּינָל

21

cold wind rests outside

there is no work to be done

the robin still sings

רוּחַ קָרִיר נָח
לֹא נוֹתְרָה עוֹד עֲבוֹדָה
הַזָּמִיר עוֹד שָׁר

22

she talks of horses

i fly west to see her ride

each plane a saddle

שָׂחָה עַל סוּסִים
טָס לִרְאוֹת רְכִיבָתָהּ
כָּל מָטוֹס אֻכָּף

23

let us be flowers

the garden is amusing

laughter is blooming

נִהְיֶה כַּפְּרָחִים

הַגַּן כֹּה מְשַׁעֲשֵׁעַ

הַצְּחוֹק פּוֹרֵחַ

24

all the leaves fall down

nature is a green scrapbook

the fires will come soon

הֶעָלִים נוֹשְׁרִים

הַטֶּבַע פִּנְקָס יָרֹק

שְׂרֵפוֹת מִתְקָרְבוֹת

25

we have become fog

so senseless is everything

we walk into walls

אָנוּ עֲרָפֶל
הַכֹּל חֲסַר תּוֹחֶלֶת
נִתְקָעִים בַּקִּיר

26

outside my window

the wind looks for my front door

it knocks and then runs

מִבַּעַד לַחַלּוֹן
רוּחַ מְחַפֶּשֶׂת דֶּלֶת
דּוֹפֶקֶת, רָצָה

27

sickness in the air

we are afraid of dying

find joy in living

חֹלִי בַּאֲוִיר
אָנוּ מְפַחֲדִים לָמוּת
רַק שְׂמַח בְּחַיֶּיךָ

28

leap into beyond

the seasons change with each breath

there is nothing here

זַנֵּק קָדִימָה
עוֹנוֹת שׁוֹנוֹת בַּנְּשִׁימוֹת
הֲלֹא כְּלוּם נוֹתָר

29

gray skies between friends
feel the deep fog between us
birds no longer sing

רָקִיעַ אָפֹר
חוּשׁ עֲרָפֶל בֵּינֵנוּ
צִפּוֹר לֹא תָּשִׁיר

30

oh meditation
tell me where the sunrise goes
I exhale the dark

הוֹ מֶדִיטַצְיָה
אָנָה פָּנְתָה הַשְּׁקִיעָה
נוֹשֵׁף חֲשֵׁכָה

31

we live in small rooms

gardens outside have windows

trees know how to stretch

חֲדָרִים צָרִים
לַגִּנּוֹת יֵשׁ חַלּוֹנוֹת
עֵצִים מִתְמַמְתְּחִים

32

i hear the silence

is that trane playing next door

listen to the rain

שׁוֹמֵעַ דְּמָמָה
טְרֵיין מְנַגֵּן לְיָדִי
הַקְשֵׁב לַגֶּשֶׁם

33

smokey robinson

the weather is turning warm

oh my girl is here

סְמוֹקִי רוֹבִּינְסוֹן
הָאֲוִיר אָז מִתְחַמֵּם
נַעֲרָתִי פֹּה

34

where does the moon go

i can only see mountains

what is beyond life

אָנָה פָּנָה לוֹ
הַסַּהַר מֵעֵבֶר לְהַר
מָה יֵשׁ מֵעֵבֶר

35

so homeless the home

there is nowhere to go to

love a resting place

כֹּה חֲסַר בַּיִת
הַבַּיִת וְאֵין לְאָן לָבֹא
נוּחַ בְּאַהֲבָה

36

sweeping the yard now

the sound of the broom singing

back and forth we go

נְקוּי הֶחָצֵר
צְלִיל שֶׁל הַמַּטְאֲטֵא שָׁר
אָנוּ לְשָׁם וּלְפֹה

37

climbing the mountain
i leave everything behind
where is my one friend

לְטַפֵּס הָרִים
הַכֹּל נוֹתַר מֵאָחוֹר
אֵיפֹה יְדִידִי

38

the last days of spring
the sun will soon burn our flesh
the joy of blackness

סוֹף הָאָבִיב בָּא
שֶׁמֶשׁ בִּשָׂרֵנוּ תִּשְׂרֹף
שִׂמְחַת הַשָּׁחוֹר

39

fear is just a door

outside there are no boundaries

stand tall like the trees

אֵין פַּחַד אֶלָּא
שַׁעַר, שָׁם בַּחוּץ אֵין סוֹף
עֲמֹד כְּמוֹ עֵצִים

40

you are not alone

the birds are calling your name

they sound like dolphy

אֵין אַתָּה בּוֹדֵד
צִיפּוֹרִים שָׁרוֹת שְׁמֶךָ
צְלִיל כְּמוֹ דוֹלְפִי

41

home is my backyard
i wait for my visitors
nature always knocks

הַבַּיִת הוּא חָצֵר
מְחַכֶּה לַמְּבַקְּרִים
הַטֶּבַע נוֹקֵשׁ

42

light inside the dark
hope is a robin singing
let us find our wings

אוֹר מֵחֲשֵׁכָה
אָדֹם חָזֶה שָׁר תִּקְוָה
נִפְרֹשׂ כְּנָפַיִם

43

will the clouds now die

parents hold their dreams dear

still they disappear

הַאִם עָנָן מֵת
הוֹרִים חֲלוֹם אוֹחֲזִים
וַחֲלוֹם אוֹבֵד

44

raccoons in daytime

are they escaping the night

hungry is the soul

דְּבִיבוֹן בַּבֹּקֶר
הַאִם מִלֵּיל הֵם בּוֹרְחִים
נֶפֶשׁ רְעֵבָה

45

where is the buddha
i find myself inside you
let the lotus speak

אֵיפֹה הַבּוּדְהַה
מוֹצֵא אֶת עַצְמִי בְּךְ
לוֹטוּס יְדַבֵּר

46

lester young leaps in
is that the frog in the pond
ben webster is here

לֶסְטֶר יָאנג זִנֵּק
זֶה צְפַרְדֵּעַ בַּשְּׁלוּלִית
בֶּן וֶובְּסְטֶר הוּא כָּאן

47

april in paris

charlie parker blows his horn

mona lisa smiles

פָּרִיז בְּאַפְּרִיל

צָ׳אִרְלִי פָּארְקֶר תּוֹקֵעַ

הָלוּבְר מְחַיֵּךְ

48

fans cheer in the park

runner races home from first

why does a man slide

מָרִיעִים בַּפַּארְק

רָץ הַבַּיְתָה מֵרִאשׁוֹן

לְמָה אִישׁ מַחְלִיק

49

blue jay in my yard

the robins singing backup

i love this music

עוֹרְבַּן בֶּחָצֵר
צִפּוֹר הַשִּׁיר מְלַוּוֹת
אוֹהֵב לְהַקְשִׁיב

50

gray sky on sunday

too many people are sick

when will the storm stop

יוֹם רִאשׁוֹן אָפֹר
הֲמוֹן אֲנָשִׁים חוֹלִים
הֲיִשָׁכֵּךְ סַעַר

51

i see the dead things

small ants carry their food home

spiders block my door

הַטֶּבַע דּוֹמֵם
הַנְּמָלִים סוֹחֲבוֹת
עַכָּבִישׁ אוֹרֵב

52

solitude is here

a bird sits on the buddha

alone i watch them

הַבְּדִידוּת בְּכָל
צִפּוֹר יָשְׁבָה עַל בּוּדְהָה
מִסְתַּכֵּל לְבַד

53

sun behind a cloud

nature is a magician

up goes the curtain

עָנָן וְשֶׁמֶשׁ
מַסְתִּיר טֶבַע הַקּוֹסֵם
הַמָּסָךְ עוֹלֶה

54

see the weeping moon

now the funeral parade

how black the night is

לְבָנָה בּוֹכָה
כָּעֵת מִצְעַד הַלְּוָיָה
לַיְלָה כֹּה שָׁחֹר

55

joy in the morning

now is the time to rake leaves

death was yesterday

עֲלִיצוּת בֹּקֶר
זֶה הַזְּמַן לִגְרֹף עָלִים
הַמָּוֶת חָלַף

56

so heavy the wind

the trees are bending again

come rain lift me up

כְּבֵדָה הָרוּחַ
שׁוּב הָעֵצִים נִכְפָּפִים
הַגֶּשֶׁם יָרִים

57

i can smell the rain

white tablecloths in the sky

your kiss stains my lips

רֵיחַ הַגֶּשֶׁם

הָרָקִיעַ הִיא מִפֹּה

פִּיךְ מַכְתִּים אֶת פִּי

58

where do we come from

why do blues fall from the sky

space is a black hole

מֵאַיִן בָּאנוּ

לְמָה בלוז מִמַּעַל בָּא

חָלָל חֹר שָׁחֹר

59

basho sing to me

walk with me through this despair

sun open my eyes

שִׁיר נָא לִי בַּאשׁוֹ
לֵךְ אִתִּי תּוֹךְ הַיֵּאוּשׁ
שֶׁמֶשׁ עֵינַי פְּקַח

60

early morning walk

it seems the world is still here

black lives still matter

צַעֲדַת שַׁחַר
נִדְמֶה הָעוֹלָם עוֹד כָּאן
וּבְּלַאק לַייבז מַאטֶר

61

hello emily

we find ourselves both indoors

the war is outside

שָׁלוֹם אֱמִילִי
הִנְנוּ בִּפְנִים הַבַּיִת
מִלְחָמָה בַּחוּץ

62

nothing stops the clock

not rain not sun not moonlight

only death moves me

אֵין הָעֲצֵר זְמַן
לֹא גֶּשֶׁם אוֹ אוֹר חַמָּה
מָוֶת מוֹשְׁכֵנִי

63

so much lays me low

a knee lowers on my neck

once again i swing

הַכֹּל מְדַכֵּא

לַחַץ בֶּרֶךְ עַל צַוָּאר

שׁוּב מִתְנַדְנֵד, זָע

64

i see the silence

the cat's tail sways in sunlight

shadows everywhere

מַבִּיט בַּדְּמָמָה

בַּשֶּׁמֶשׁ יֵשׁ צֵל זָנָב

חָתוּל מְכַשְׁכֵּשׁ

65

the hunting season

black men running in circles

looking for their wings

עוֹנַת הַצַּיִד
מַעְגָּל גְּבָרִים שְׁחֹרִים
וּבְלִי כְּנָפַיִם

66

blood flows in the street

a man is a fragile thing

why do they break us

דָּם זוֹרֵם בָּרְחוֹב
אָדָם הוּא דָּבָר שָׁבִיר
לָמָּה אֲנַחְנוּ

67

dead trees in the yard

what omens fell with the leaves

a sad choir sings

עֵץ מֵת בֶּחָצֵר

מָה נִרְמַז בַּשַּׁלֶּכֶת

מַקְהֵלָה שָׁרָה

68

stop the fighting

should we blame poison ivy

let our flowers breathe

עֲצוֹר אֶת הַקְּרָב

נַאֲשִׁים אֶת הַקִּיסוֹס

תְּנוּ פְּרָחִים לִנְשֹׁם

69

night comes through windows
a bed is where all dreams sleep
the stars are naked

לַיְלָה בַּחַלּוֹן
בְּמִטָּה יָשֵׁן חֲלוֹם
הַכּוֹכָב עָרוֹם

70

thunderstorms crying
what is rain but our sorrows
why is grief so loud

הָרְעָמִים בּוֹכִים
גֶּשֶׁם הוּא צַעֲרֵנוּ
יָגוֹן בְּקוֹל רַעַם

71

dead leaves surround me

i mourn the darkness of days

so black the green woods

סָבִיב רַק רָקָב
מַסְפִּיד יָמִים אֲפֵלִים
הַחֹרֶשׁ שָׁחֹר

72

flying fish don't fly

they only swim through the air

blue wind splashing

דָּגִים לֹא עָפִים
אֶלָּא שׂוֹחִים בָּאֲוִיר
תְּכֹל הָרוּחַ לַח

73

sunlight on a chair

books of poetry waiting

eyes on the bookshelf

קֶרֶן עַל כִּסֵּא
סִפְרֵי שִׁירָה מְחַכִּים
מַבָּט אֶל מַדָּף

74

so loud the silence

in the morning birds whisper

open the window

דְּמָמָה רוֹעֶשֶׁת
בַּבֹּקֶר צִפּוֹר לוֹחֵשׁ
פְּתַח אֶת הַחַלּוֹן

75

water in a bowl

can love escape desire

too much spills each day

מַיִם בַּקְּעָרָה
בְּרַח אוֹהֵב מִתְּשׁוּקָתְךָ
הֵצֶף יוֹמְיוֹמִי

76

the white fog lifting

can you see the road ahead

where did we come from

עֲרָפֶּל לָבָן
הַדֶּרֶךְ לְפָנֵינוּ
מֵאַיִן בָּאנוּ

77

the trees are falling

the sand is disappearing

there is nothing left

הָעֵצִים נוֹפְלִים
הַחוֹלוֹת נֶעֱלָמִים
דָּבָר לֹא נוֹתַר

78

inhale the blueness

we are flies trapped inside rooms

our wings are useless

נְשֹׁם אֶת הַכָּחֹל
כִּזְבוּב נָעוּל בַּחֶדֶר
לְשֵׁם מָה כְּנָפַיִם

79

nobody is home

paint peeling off the front door

weeds cutting the grass

אֵין כָּאן אַף אֶחָד
קָלוּף צֶבַע בַּדֶּלֶת
דֶּשֶׁא מִשְׁתַּטֵּה

80

birds searching for food

death has such beautiful wings

each day we struggle

עוֹף אַחַר מָזוֹן
כָּנָף נָאֶה לְמָוֶת
עֵת לְמַאֲבָק

81

the body breaks down

hold the earthquake in your hands

pieces of a man

הַגּוּף מִתְמוֹטֵט
שִׁמְרוּ רַעַשׁ בְּיֶדְכֶם
חֲתִיכוֹת אָדָם

82

who cut the bushes

hide the obituaries

black lives are too short

הַגּוֹזֵם שִׂיחַ
אַל נָא תַּסְפִּיד, הַשָּׁחֹר
חַיָּיו כֹּה קְצָרִים

83

when will the words come

i wait for the fruit to fall

so sweet are the poems

בּוֹאוּ הַמִּלִּים
עֵת אַמְתִּין שֶׁיַּבְשִׁיל פְּרִי
שִׁירִים יִמְתָּקוּ

84

sorrow does not last

there is joy in the morning

light will find a way

הַצַּעַר חוֹלֵף
הַשַּׁחַר עוֹלֶה, הָאוֹר
אֶת דַּרְכּוֹ יִמְצָא

85

waiting for the night

how soon can i pay my rent

the blues never sleeps

הַלַּיְלָה עוֹד בָּא
מָה מוֹעֵד שְׂכַר הַדִּירָה
לֹא יָנוּם הַבְּלוּז

86

feathers are like days

youth is known to fly away

so hungry the bird

הַנּוֹצוֹת כְּיָמִים
יָדוּעַ שֶׁנֹּעַר עָף
צִפּוֹר מְרֻעֶבֶת

87

the smell of morning

let another day touch you

where are you going

רֵיחַ הַבֹּקֶר

תֵּן לְעוֹד יוֹם לָגַעַת

אָז לְאָן הוֹלְכִים

88

where is my jazz hat

the one that monk used to wear

oh ruby my dear

כּוֹבַע גֵ׳׳ז שֶׁלִּי

זֶה שֶׁמוֹנְק הָיָה חוֹבֵשׁ

רוּבִּי יְקָרָה

89

death don't make me cry

here come the saints marching in

lord play your trumpet

מָוֶת בְּלִי יָגוֹן

בַּסַּךְ קְדוֹשִׁים יִצְעָדוּ

תְּהֵה תְּרוּעַת אֵל

90

don't close the window

let us breathe the very sweet air

bring the love indoors

פְּתַח אֶת הַחַלּוֹן

בּוֹא וְנִנְשֹׁם מְתִיקוּת

אַהֲבָה פְּנִימָה

91

can you taste that jazz

satchmo laughing through his horn

oh– red beans and rice

תִּטְעַם אֶת הַגֶ'ז
סָצְ'מוֹ צוֹחֵק בְּקַרְנוֹ
הוֹ! שְׁעוּעִית וְאֹרֶז

92

blowin in the wind

a young dylan sings to us

we still need answers

עָפָה בָּרוּחַ
שָׁר לָנוּ דִּילָן צָעִיר
וּתְשׁוּבָה אֵין לִי

93

can you hear the heart

the poor sit holding blankets

don't your hands still see

הָאֹזֶן לַלֵּב
אוֹחֵז עָנִי בְּסְדִינָיו,
אֵין יָדְךָ רוֹאָה?

94

lewis on a bridge

the police mob attacking

one cannot club change

לוּאִיס עַל גֶּשֶׁר
הֲמוֹן הַשׁוֹטְרִים תֹּקֵף
אֵין בְּאַלּוֹת שִׁנּוּי

95

keep looking for signs

open the book of nature

talk with the flowers

חַפֵּשׂ סִימָנִים
פְּתַח אֶת סֵפֶר הַטֶּבַע
דַּבֵּר עִם פְּרָחִים

96

the days are not dark

we have been sleeping too long

rise and bring the light

אֵין הַיּוֹם אָפֵל
יָשַׁנּוּ זְמַן רַב מִדַּי
קוּם הָבֵא הָאוֹר

97

our world has collapsed

we now dance with earthquakes

we are moved by fear

הָעוֹלָם קָרַס

בּוֹא נִרְקֹד עִם הָרַעַשׁ

הַפַּחַד מַרְטִיט

98

the days disappear

alone we return to earth

the long sleep ahead

הַיָּמִים חוֹלְפִים

חוֹזְרִים לַקַּרְקַע לַבַּד

שֵׁנָה אֲרֻכָּה

99

it's almost august

i need to hold summer close

let's sweat while we love

כְּבָר אוֹגוּסְט עוֹד מְעַט

מַחֲזִיק קַיִץ קָרוֹב

נֹאהַב נַזִּיעַ

100

we live with our luck

every day we must struggle

our black lives matter

טִפָּה שֶׁל מַזָּל

אַךְ כָּל יוֹם אָנוּ סוֹבְלִים

וּבְלַאק לַייבז מַאטֶר

101

a storm is coming

why do our fears fear the wind

what rain brings a knife

הַסּוּפָה קְרֵבָה

רוּחַ תַּפְחִיד פַּחַד, יֵשׁ

לַגֶּשֶׁם לַהַב

102

when will the fog lift

how do i find the right path

look beyond the veil

עֲרָפֶל נָסוֹג כָּבֵד

מַהִי דַּרְכִּי לְאָן אֵלֵךְ

בְּלִי הַהִינוּמָה

103

underneath the masks

the world is suffocating

our fears are flowering

תַּחַת מַסֵּכוֹת

הָעוֹלָם אַט וְנֶחֱנַק

פְּרִיחַת הַפַּחַד

104

horn lips cherry red

legs sway under a table

jazz will seduce you

שָׂפָה דֻּבְדְּבָן

רֶטֶט נִסְתָּר שֶׁל רֶגֶל

פִּתּוּיֵי הַגַ׳ז

105

sitting in the dark

one cannot see the future

where is the candle

יוֹשְׁבִים בַּחֹשֶׁךְ

הֶעָתִיד בִּלְתִּי נִרְאָה

הַנֵּר אֵינֶנּוּ

106

we invent ourselves

the soul is never perfect

change can be plastic

אָנוּ הִמְצֵאָנוּ

אֵין בַּנֶּפֶשׁ שְׁלֵמוּת כְּלָל

שִׁנּוּי מִפְּלַסְטִיק

53

107

people need the wood

do not carry a large cross

resurrect yourself

נִזְקָקִים לָעֵץ
הָסִירוּ מַשָּׂא הַצְּלָב
תִּחְיֶה וְתִחְיֶה

108

the weather is cool

see sinatra tip his hat

fly me to the moon

הָאֲוִיר קָרִיר
כּוֹבָעוֹ שֶׁל סִינָטְרָה
טָס לַיָּרֵחַ

109

oh thelonious

lightning strikes the piano

rain falls full of notes

הוֹ! הוֹ! תֶּ׳לוֹנְיוּס

בָּרָק מַכֶּה בַּפְּסַנְתֵּר

מָטָר שֶׁל תָּוִים

110

cool jazz on my skin

the days of august over

let's dance until dawn

קוּל גֵ׳'ז עַל עוֹרִי

יְמֵי אוֹגוּסְט אָז חָלְפוּ

נִרְקֹד עַד שָׁחַר

111

big man with a bass

look beneath the underdog

it's always mingus

אִישׁ גָּדוֹל, בַּטְנוּן

עִם עֶמְדָּה נְמוּכָה

זֶה תָּמִיד מִנְגּוּס

112

music in a cage

free jazz and ornette coleman

notes fly from his horn

מוּסִיקָה בַּכְּלוּב

פְּרִי גֵ׳ז וְאָרְנֶט קוֹלְמָן

תָּוִים מְקַרְנוֹ

113

time to get away

sun ra is no longer here

yes space is the place

הַזְּמַן לִבְרֹחַ
סַאן רָא עוֹד לֹא נִמְצָא כָּאן
חָלָל זֶה מָקוֹם

114

the sound of music

let's dance to the count and duke

royalty is here

צְלִיל הַמּוּסִיקָה
נִרְקֹד לִפְנֵי קָאוֹנְט וְדִיּוּק
הַמְּלוּכָה הִיא כָּאן

115

are you kind of blue

miles is boxing with his horn

i hear jack johnson

הַאִם אַתְּ מִין בְּלוּ

מָיְלְס מִתְאַגְרֵף עִם קַרְנוֹ

מַקְשִׁיב לְג׳וֹנְסוֹן

116

my head in a cloud

i have gray sky and blue thoughts

the grass needs cutting

רָאשִׁי בֶּעָנָן

אָפֹר מֵעַל בְּלוּ בָּרֹאשׁ

דֶּשֶׁא לֹא גָזוּם

117

blue chill in the air

bovey turns her head away

who can we flirt with

אוֹר תְּכֵלֶת קָרָה
בּוֹוִיי מַפְנָה אֶת רֹאשָׁהּ
עִם מִי נְפְלַרְטֵט

118

june jumps off a cliff

summer rises with the heat

so cold the graveyard

גֹ'וּן קָפְצָה מִצּוּק
זְרִיחַת הַקַּיִץ וְחוֹמוֹ
צִנַּת הַקְּבָרִים

119

do you hear the wind

alice coltrane plays her harp

finger the music

הֲתִשְׁמַע מַשָּׁב
אָלִיס קוֹלְטְרֵין בַּנֵּבֶל
נִפְרַט הַמֵּיתָר

120

Let's forget the past.

Don't think about the future.

Oh now is the time

שְׁכַח מִן הֶעָבָר
לֹא נַחְשֹׁב עַל הֶעָתִיד
עֵת לִזְמַן הֹוֶה

about the authors

E. Ethelbert Miller is a literary activist and author of two memoirs and several poetry collections. He hosts the WPFW morning radio show *On the Margin with E. Ethelbert Miller* and hosts and produces *The Scholars* on UDC-TV which received a 2020 Telly Award. Miller is Associate Editor and a columnist for The American Book Review. He was given a 2020 congressional award from Congressman Jamie Raskin in recognition of his literary activism, awarded the 2022 *Howard Zinn Lifetime Achievement Award* by the Peace and Justice Studies Association, and named a 2023 Grammy Nominee Finalist for Best Spoken Word Poetry Album. Miller's latest book is *How I Found Love Behind the Catcher's Mask*, published by City Point Press.

Rafi Ellenson is a poet and literary translator based in Somerville, MA studying towards rabbinical ordination at the Rabbinical School of Hebrew College. His writing has previously been published in *Verklempt!* and *Jewish Currents*. This is his first book.

acknowledgments

Joanna Chen and Raz Chen-Morris
Kate Damon
Barbara Goldberg
Miho Kinnas
Merrill Leffler
Lenard Moore